Table of contents

The complete pocket guide to Crypto Investment – Everything you need to know 2
Why understanding the basics of crypto investing important? 2
1. Background and History of Cryptocurrency...3
2. Understanding Blockchain Technology..4
3. Popular Cryptocurrencies..5
4. Setting Up a Crypto Wallet..8
5. Diving into the World of Crypto Exchanges...12
6. Crafting Your Winning Investment Strategy..13
7. Tackling the Risks and Challenges in Crypto Investing................................20
8. Mastering Taxes and Regulations in the Crypto World..................................21
9. Staying Informed and Educated – Your Key to Crypto Success..........................22
Conclusion 23

The complete pocket guide to Crypto Investment
– Everything you need to know

Welcome to the beginner's guide to investing in cryptocurrencies, where we'll demystify the world of digital assets and help you navigate the thrilling crypto landscape with ease. You might be wondering, where do we start? What factors should we consider, and how do we make sense of the complexities that come with crypto investing? Is there a way to master the art of managing cryptocurrencies while reducing risks and maximising returns?

Put simply, this guide is your go-to resource for understanding the ins and outs of investing in cryptocurrencies like Bitcoin, Ethereum, and many others. More specifically, we'll delve into the history of digital currencies, the game-changing blockchain technology, selecting the right crypto wallet and exchange, and developing a winning investment strategy. While the world of cryptocurrencies might seem daunting and intricate, there's no need to fret.

Why understanding the basics of crypto investing important?

In a nutshell, understanding the basics of crypto investing is the key to unlocking your potential in the ever-evolving digital asset landscape. More specifically, it empowers you to make informed decisions, identify potential opportunities, and navigate the intricacies of the crypto market with ease. While the realm of cryptocurrencies may appear overwhelming and convoluted, there's no need for apprehension.

By mastering the essentials of crypto investing, you'll be better equipped to manage the volatility and uncertainties associated with digital assets.

Furthermore, you'll gain insights into the revolutionary blockchain technology, allowing you to appreciate the transformative impact of cryptocurrencies on the global financial system.

Sit back, relax, and let us be your trusty companion on this exciting journey. The following sections are brimming with indispensable knowledge and practical tools to help you get a firm grasp of cryptocurrency investing and best practices. Prepare to embark on a thrilling adventure into the realm of digital assets!

1. Background and History of Cryptocurrency

– How exactly did it begin?

Let's take a trip down memory lane to the early 1980s, when ingenious cryptographers and computer scientists first toyed with the concept of digital currencies. The crypto revolution truly kicked off in 2008, when an enigmatic individual or group known as Satoshi Nakamoto unveiled a white paper on Bitcoin. This groundbreaking document outlined the design and functionality of the world's first cryptocurrency. In 2009, the first Bitcoin transaction took place, and the age of cryptocurrencies was born.

From that moment on, the crypto industry skyrocketed, with a myriad of digital currencies bursting onto the scene. Bitcoin remains the most famous and valuable cryptocurrency, but other influential players like Ethereum, Ripple (XRP), and Litecoin have also captured the world's attention.

The driving force behind cryptocurrencies is the longing for a decentralised financial system, empowering users to manage their assets independently of intermediaries like banks or financial institutions. This decentralisation is made possible by blockchain technology, the backbone of most cryptocurrencies, ensuring their security, transparency, and immutability.

2. Understanding Blockchain Technology

Picture blockchain technology as the bedrock of cryptocurrencies, offering a decentralised ledger that meticulously records transactions. A blockchain is a chain of interconnected blocks, each housing a cluster of transactions. Once a block is verified and connected to the chain, its data is set in stone, safeguarding the integrity of the information.

The decentralised nature of blockchain technology is its crowning glory. Instead of being governed by a single authority, a blockchain is upheld by a network of computers, known as nodes. These nodes collaborate to validate and confirm transactions, adding new blocks to the chain. This teamwork eliminates the need for intermediaries and guarantees that no single entity can tamper with the data.

Such distributed system of validation makes blockchain technology incredibly secure and transparent. Each node in the network holds a copy of the blockchain, meaning that if one node fails or is compromised, the others continue to maintain the integrity of the ledger. This also ensures that the system is tamper-proof, as any attempt to alter data in one block would require consensus from the entire network, making fraudulent activity nearly impossible.

Moreover, blockchain technology is not just limited to cryptocurrencies. Its decentralised, transparent and secure nature can be used in a wide range of applications, from supply chain management to voting systems. By providing a tamper-proof, shared database, blockchain technology can enable more trust, accountability and efficiency in many industries.

3. Popular Cryptocurrencies

Among the thousands of cryptocurrencies, some of the most renowned ones are:

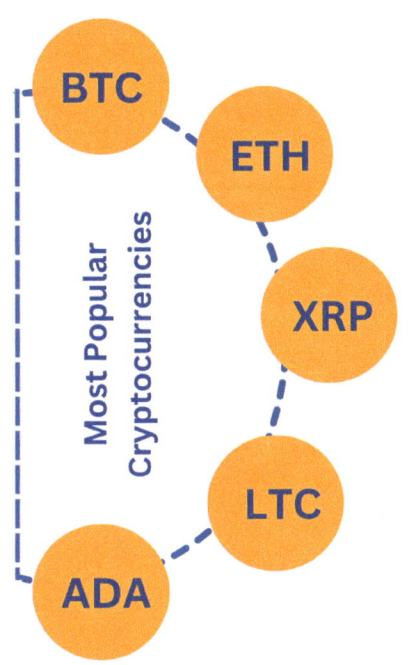

- **Bitcoin (BTC)**: Frequently dubbed "digital gold," Bitcoin is the pioneer and most valuable cryptocurrency. Its primary purpose is as a store of value and medium of exchange.

- **Ethereum (ETH):** Ethereum is a platform for crafting decentralised applications (dApps) and smart contracts. Its native currency, Ether, fuels these applications and is the second-largest cryptocurrency by market cap.

- **Ripple (XRP):** Ripple's mission is to enable swift, cost-effective cross-border transactions by connecting banks, payment providers, and digital asset exchanges. XRP is the native currency utilised within the Ripple network.

- **Litecoin (LTC):** Referred to as "silver to Bitcoin's gold," Litecoin is a nimbler and more scalable alternative to Bitcoin, designed for everyday transactions.

- **Cardano (ADA):** Cardano is a smart contract platform aiming to deliver a more scalable and energy-efficient solution compared to Ethereum. Its native currency, ADA, is used for transactions and securing the network.

Each cryptocurrency boasts unique features, technology, and applications. When investing, it's vital to research and comprehend the underlying technology and potential uses of each digital asset.

Let's have a closer look.

- Bitcoin (BTC)

Technology: Bitcoin operates on a decentralised, permissionless blockchain, utilising a Proof of Work (PoW) consensus mechanism. The network is supported by miners, who validate transactions and maintain the blockchain's integrity.

Use Cases: Bitcoin's primary use case is as a digital store of value and a medium of exchange. It's often referred to as "digital gold" due to its limited supply and deflationary nature. Bitcoin also enables cross-border transactions and serves as a hedge against inflation and currency devaluation.

- Ethereum (ETH)

Technology: Ethereum is a decentralised, open-source blockchain platform that enables the creation of smart contracts and decentralised applications (dApps). It uses a PoW consensus mechanism, with plans to transition to Proof of Stake (PoS) through Ethereum 2.0.

Use Cases: Ethereum's primary use case is to serve as the foundation for building dApps, enabling decentralised finance (DeFi), non-fungible tokens (NFTs), and a plethora of other applications. ETH, its native cryptocurrency, is also used for transactions, gas fees, and staking.

- Ripple (XRP)

Technology: Ripple's underlying technology, the XRP Ledger, is a decentralised, permissionless blockchain that uses a consensus protocol called the Ripple Protocol Consensus Algorithm (RPCA). It offers fast and low-cost transactions compared to traditional financial systems.

Use Cases: Ripple's primary use case is to facilitate cross-border transactions and remittances, offering a more efficient alternative to traditional financial systems. XRP, its native cryptocurrency, acts as a bridge currency between different fiat currencies, enabling near-instant transactions.

- Litecoin (LTC)

Technology: Litecoin is a decentralised, open-source cryptocurrency that operates on a PoW blockchain similar to Bitcoin. However, it employs the Scrypt hashing algorithm, which allows for faster transaction processing and lower fees.

Use Cases: Litecoin's main use case is as a digital currency for everyday transactions, often dubbed as the "silver to Bitcoin's gold." It's designed for faster, cheaper transactions and aims to complement Bitcoin as an alternative payment option.

- Cardano (ADA)

Technology: Cardano is a decentralised, open-source blockchain platform that uses a PoS consensus mechanism called Ouroboros. It's built with a strong emphasis on research and peer-review, aiming to achieve a high level of scalability, security, and sustainability.

Use Cases: Cardano's primary use case is to serve as a platform for building smart contracts and dApps. It aims to tackle issues related to scalability, interoperability, and sustainability in the blockchain space. ADA, its native cryptocurrency, is used for transactions, staking, and governance.

4. Setting Up a Crypto Wallet

A crypto wallet is a nifty tool that allows you to store, send, and receive cryptocurrencies safely. There are several wallet types to choose from:

•**Hardware wallets:** Physical devices that store your private keys offline, offering top-notch security. Examples include Ledger and Trezor.

(*Ledger Nano X Crypto Hardware Wallet displayed on the left*)

Pros:

- Excellent security features, such as private key storage offline and two-factor authentication.
- Immune to computer viruses and malware attacks.
- Can store a wide range of cryptocurrencies.

Cons:

- Higher upfront cost compared to software wallets.
- May require a learning curve to use effectively.
- If lost or damaged, it can be challenging to recover the funds.

•**Software wallets:** Applications that can be installed on your computer or smartphone, providing a balance of security and convenience. Examples include Exodus and MyEtherWallet.

Pros:

- Convenient and easy to use.
- Often free or low-cost.
- Available on a wide range of devices, including desktop and mobile.

Cons:

- Potentially more susceptible to hacking and malware attacks than hardware wallets.
- Security may depend on the device it is installed on.
- May have limitations on the types of cryptocurrencies it can store.

- **Custodial wallets:** Wallets offered by cryptocurrency exchanges or third parties that store your private keys on their servers. While user-friendly, you're trusting your assets to the service provider.

Pros:

- Easy to use, as the provider manages the security and maintenance of the wallet.
- Often have insurance to protect against losses.

Cons:

- Reliance on third-party provider to manage your assets.
- Limited control over your private keys and funds.
- May be vulnerable to hacking and security breaches.

When selecting a wallet, consider factors like security, ease of use, and compatibility with the cryptocurrencies you intend to invest in. Don't forget to follow best practices for securing your wallet, such as backing up your private keys, enabling two-factor authentication, and keeping your software up to date.

Setting Up a Hardware Crypto Wallet

Step 1: Choose a reputable hardware wallet brand, such as Ledger, Trezor, or KeepKey. Research the features, compatibility, and pricing to determine the best option for your needs.

Step 2: Purchase your chosen hardware wallet from the official manufacturer's website or a trusted retailer to ensure authenticity.

Step 3: Connect the wallet to your computer or mobile device using the provided cable or adapter. Follow the manufacturer's instructions to install any necessary software or apps.

Step 4: Create a new wallet by following the on-screen prompts. The wallet will generate a unique seed phrase, typically consisting of 12, 18, or 24 words. Write down the seed phrase and store it in a secure location, as it's the only way to recover your wallet if the device is lost or damaged.

Step 5: Set a strong PIN to protect your wallet from unauthorised access.

Step 6: Your hardware wallet is now set up and ready to use. You can send, receive, and manage your cryptocurrencies through the wallet's interface.

Setting Up a Software Crypto Wallet

Step 1: Research and choose a reputable software wallet compatible with your chosen cryptocurrencies and device, such as Exodus, Electrum, or Mycelium.

Step 2: Download and install the wallet software from the official website or app store.

Step 3: Launch the wallet and create a new wallet by following the on-screen prompts.

Step 4: The wallet will generate a unique seed phrase, usually consisting of 12, 18, or 24 words. Write down the seed phrase and store it in a secure location, as it's essential for wallet recovery.

Step 5: Set a strong password or PIN to protect your wallet from unauthorised access.

Step 6: Your software wallet is now set up and ready to use. You can send, receive, and manage your cryptocurrencies through the wallet's interface.

Setting Up a Custodial Crypto Wallet

Step 1: Choose a reputable custodial wallet service, such as Coinbase, Binance, or Gemini. Research the features, fees, and security measures to determine the best option for your needs.

Step 2: Register for an account with the custodial wallet provider. You may be required to provide personal information and verify your identity, depending on the provider's Know Your Customer (KYC) requirements.

Step 3: Set a strong password for your account and enable two-factor authentication (2FA) for added security.

Step 4: Once your account is set up and verified, you can deposit, withdraw, and manage your cryptocurrencies using the provider's platform.

Remember, the security of your cryptocurrencies is paramount. Always research your options and follow best practices to ensure the safe storage and management of your digital assets.

5. Diving into the World of Crypto Exchanges

To buy, sell, or trade cryptocurrencies, you'll need to explore the realm of crypto exchanges. These platforms come in various shapes and sizes, offering different features and fees.

There are 3 main types of exchanges to choose from:

1. Centralised exchanges: These popular exchanges act as intermediaries between buyers and sellers, with examples such as Coinbase, Binance, and Kraken.

> Coinbase: User-friendly and widely popular, Coinbase is an excellent starting point for beginners. It supports a variety of cryptocurrencies and provides a simple interface.
>
> Binance: As one of the largest exchanges by trading volume, Binance offers an extensive range of cryptocurrencies and advanced trading features.
>
> Kraken: Known for its strong security measures, Kraken is a popular choice for traders who prioritise safety. The platform also supports fiat currency deposits and withdrawals.

2. Decentralised exchanges (DEX): These platforms enable peer-to-peer trading without a central authority, utilising smart contracts to execute trades. Examples include Uniswap and PancakeSwap.

3. Peer-to-peer (P2P) exchanges: These platforms directly connect buyers and sellers, allowing them to negotiate their trade terms. Examples include LocalBitcoins and Paxful.

When selecting an exchange, keep in mind factors like security, fees, supported cryptocurrencies, and user-friendliness. Additionally, double-check the exchange's reputation and regulatory compliance to guarantee a safe and seamless trading experience.

6. Crafting Your Winning Investment Strategy

Now that you're acquainted with the basics, it's time to design your solid investment strategy that aligns with your risk tolerance and financial goals.

Here are some key aspects to consider:

1. Diversify — Spread your investments across multiple cryptocurrencies and asset classes to minimise risk.

2. Research — Conduct thorough research on each cryptocurrency before investing. Understand the technology, team, and use cases behind each digital asset.

3. Set Goals — Outline your short-term and long-term objectives, such as capital growth, income generation, or portfolio diversification.

4. Stay informed — Keep up with the latest news, developments, and trends in the crypto industry to make informed investment decisions.

5. Strategise — Contemplate different approaches, like dollar-cost averaging (investing a fixed amount regularly) or lump-sum investing (investing a substantial sum at once).

6. Start Small

7. Be Patient

Invest only what you can afford to lose, and gradually increase your investments as you gain experience and confidence.

Cryptocurrency markets can be volatile. Stay patient and stick to your investment strategy, resisting the urge to make impulsive decisions based on short-term market fluctuations.

1. Master the Art of **Diversification**

Just as in traditional investing, diversification is a crucial component of a successful crypto investment strategy. Spreading your investments across a variety of digital assets reduces the impact of any single asset's poor performance on your overall portfolio. By diversifying, you're not putting all your eggs in one basket, mitigating the risk and enhancing your potential for rewards.

To achieve a well-diversified crypto portfolio, consider investing in a mix of established cryptocurrencies like Bitcoin (BTC) and Ethereum (ETH), as well as newer, promising projects with solid fundamentals. You may also want to explore different sectors within the crypto ecosystem, such as decentralised finance (DeFi), non-fungible tokens (NFTs), and blockchain infrastructure projects.

In the fast-paced world of crypto investing, having a solid risk management plan is essential to protect your hard-earned capital and maximise your profits. A well-designed risk management strategy helps you identify, assess, and address potential risks associated with your investments, ensuring that you're prepared for any unexpected market turbulence.

Some **key components of** an effective **risk management** plan include:

- Setting stop-loss orders to automatically sell an asset if its price drops below a predetermined level, limiting your losses in case of a market downturn.
- Establishing clear profit-taking targets, allowing you to lock in gains when your investments perform well.
- Regularly reviewing and adjusting your portfolio allocation to maintain an optimal balance of risk and reward.

2. Top Strategy for Thorough **Research**

To make informed decisions and minimise risks in the crypto market, conducting thorough research on each cryptocurrency is essential.

Here's a Step-by-Step strategy to help you gain a deeper understanding of the technology, team, and use cases behind each digital asset:

A. **Study the project's white-paper:**
   The white-paper is a foundational document that outlines the project's goals, technology, tokenomics, and roadmap. Pay attention to the problem the project aims to solve, how it plans to achieve this, and the uniqueness of its solution.

B. **Analyse the underlying technology:**
   Dive into the technical aspects of the project, including the blockchain platform, consensus mechanism, and scalability. Ensure the technology is robust, secure, and innovative.

C. **Evaluate the project's team and advisors:**
   A competent team and experienced advisors are crucial for a project's success. Investigate the background of key team members, their expertise, and previous accomplishments in the blockchain or tech industry.

D. **Assess token utility and use cases:**
   Understand the role of the project's native token within its ecosystem, and explore its potential use cases. A token with a clear purpose and real-world applications is more likely to succeed.

E. **Review the project's roadmap and progress:**
   Evaluate the project's progress by comparing its roadmap with actual achievements. A project that consistently meets its milestones is more likely to deliver on its promises.

F. **Monitor community sentiment and engagement:**
   Analyse the project's online presence and community engagement on social media, forums, and chat platforms. A strong, active community can be an indicator of a project's potential success.

G. **Examine the project's market performance:**
   Review the token's historical price, trading volume, and market capitalisation. Analyse the performance of similar projects in the market to identify trends and potential growth.

3. Set Your **Goals** Right

Establishing clear objectives is essential for crafting a successful investment plan.

Here's a <u>Strategy</u> to help you outline your short-term and long-term goals:

A. **Identify your investment priorities**:
   Determine whether you seek capital growth, income generation, or portfolio diversification. Consider your financial situation, risk tolerance, and investment horizon when setting your priorities.

B. **Set specific, measurable, and time-bound goals**:
   Create quantifiable objectives with clear timeframes. For instance, you might aim to achieve a 10% return on investment within one year or double your investment within five years.

C. **Monitor your progress**:
   Regularly review your portfolio performance to track your progress towards your goals. Adjust your strategy as needed to ensure you remain on target.

4. Stay **Informed** and **Adapt** to Market Changes

The cryptocurrency market is known for its rapid pace and frequent changes, making it vital for investors to stay informed and adapt their strategies accordingly. By keeping up-to-date with the latest news, trends, and developments in the crypto space, you can make better-informed investment decisions and respond effectively to market shifts.

5. Embrace the Power of **DCA & LSI**

Dollar-cost averaging (DCA) is a time-tested investment strategy that involves consistently investing a fixed amount of money at regular intervals, regardless of market conditions. This approach allows you to build a position in an asset over time while mitigating the effects of market volatility.

By employing a DCA strategy, you avoid the pitfalls of trying to time the market and reduce the risk of making poor investment decisions based on emotions or short-term fluctuations. As a result, you accumulate cryptocurrencies at an average price over time, smoothing out the highs and lows of the market.

To implement a dollar-cost averaging strategy in your crypto investing journey, decide on a fixed amount you're comfortable investing regularly, and commit to buying your chosen cryptocurrencies at set intervals, such as weekly or monthly.

Lump-sum investing (LSI) is a powerful approach that involves investing a significant amount of money in a single transaction, capitalising on the potential for long-term growth. This strategy leverages the concept of time in the market, allowing your investment to benefit from compounding returns and market appreciation over an extended period.

By opting for a lump-sum investment, you seize the opportunity to maximise your returns by taking advantage of the market's upward trajectory. Instead of waiting for the perfect entry point, you commit your capital to the market, giving it ample time to grow and prosper.

To effectively execute a lump-sum investing strategy in your crypto journey, carefully assess your financial situation and determine an appropriate sum of money to invest. Then, allocate your capital across a diverse range of cryptocurrencies and asset classes, taking into consideration your risk tolerance and investment objectives. Once your investment is in place, focus on long-term growth and avoid being swayed by short-term market fluctuations or emotional reactions to market events.

6. Start **Small** and Gradually **Increase**

As you become more comfortable and knowledgeable in the crypto market, you may wish to gradually increase your investments.

Here's a <u>Strategy</u> to help you achieve this:

A. **Start small:**
   Begin with a modest investment in a few well-established cryptocurrencies. This approach allows you to test the waters and gain experience without significant risk.

B. **Learn from experience:**
   Track your investment performance and analyse your successes and failures. Use this insight to refine your strategy and decision-making process.

C. **Educate yourself:**
   Continuously expand your knowledge of the crypto market, blockchain technology, and investment strategies. Stay informed about industry trends, news, and developments.

D. **Reinvest profits:**
   Consider reinvesting a portion of your gains to increase your investment capital. This approach allows you to compound your returns and potentially grow your wealth faster.

E. **Diversify your portfolio:**
   As you gain confidence, explore new investment opportunities, such as altcoins, DeFi projects, and ICOs. Diversify your portfolio by adding assets with different risk profiles, use cases, and market positions.

F. **Implement advanced strategies:**
   As your experience grows, experiment with advanced investment strategies, such as trading derivatives, shorting assets, or using leverage. Remember, these strategies can carry higher risks, so ensure you thoroughly understand them before proceeding.

By following this step-by-step approach, you can gradually increase your investments in the crypto market while building your experience, confidence, and knowledge. Always remember to invest responsibly, manage your risks, and continuously learn to improve your investment outcomes.

7. Be **Patient** and Stick to Your Investment Plan

One of the most critical factors for achieving long-term success in crypto investing is having the patience to stick to your investment plan. While the temptation to chase short-term gains or react to sudden market movements is natural, it's essential to stay focused on your long-term objectives and adhere to your well-defined strategy.

Developing a clear investment plan, complete with specific goals, time horizons, and risk tolerance levels, is key to maintaining discipline and resisting impulsive decisions that may harm your portfolio. By staying patient and committed to your plan, you'll be better positioned to ride out market volatility and achieve long-term success.

Bottom Line

Maximising your profits in the dynamic world of crypto investing requires a combination of bold strategies and prudent decision-making. By diversifying your portfolio, employing dollar-cost averaging, developing a robust risk management plan, staying informed about market changes, and practicing patience, you'll be well on your way to unlocking the full potential of this exciting asset class.

Remember, the key to success in crypto investing lies in continuous learning, staying informed, and adapting your strategies to ever-evolving market conditions. By following these guidelines and staying committed to ongoing education, you'll be well-equipped to navigate the thrilling crypto landscape and achieve maximum profits in your investment journey.

7. Tackling the Risks and Challenges in Crypto Investing

Crypto investing, like any financial venture, comes with its unique set of risks and challenges that you should be aware of:

Market volatility: In the world of cryptocurrencies, prices can experience significant fluctuations in a short period. While this might seem daunting, understanding the market trends will help you make more informed decisions and potentially benefit from these changes.

Security concerns: The digital nature of cryptocurrencies makes them susceptible to hacking, phishing attacks, and other security threats. But fear not! By following best practices to secure your wallet and private keys, you can significantly reduce the risks of loss or theft.

Regulatory issues: The legal landscape for cryptocurrencies varies by country, and government intervention can impact the market. Staying informed about regulatory developments and ensuring compliance with local laws will help you navigate this ever-changing terrain with confidence.

While crypto investing comes with its share of risks and challenges, being aware of these factors and taking the necessary precautions can help you make informed decisions and potentially reap the rewards of this exciting and rapidly evolving market.

8. Mastering Taxes and Regulations in the Crypto World

Understanding the tax implications of cryptocurrency investments is essential for proper financial planning. While this might seem like a daunting task, we're here to guide you through the process:

In many countries, cryptocurrencies are considered taxable assets, and you may be required to report your transactions, gains, and losses for tax purposes. To ensure compliance with local tax laws and regulations, consult a tax professional or financial advisor. Additionally, maintain accurate records of your transactions, including dates, amounts, and the fair market value of the assets at the time of the transaction.

It's also crucial to stay informed about regulatory developments in the crypto space. Regulations can vary significantly by country and may change over time, so keep up-to-date with the latest news and guidelines to ensure your investments remain compliant.

9. Staying Informed and Educated – Your Key to Crypto Success

The world of cryptocurrencies is constantly evolving, and it's essential to stay informed and educated about the latest developments.

With our guidance, you'll have the tools and resources to keep up-to-date and make better investment decisions:

 •Follow reputable news sources and blogs dedicated to cryptocurrencies and blockchain technology.

 •Subscribe to newsletters, podcasts, or YouTube channels that cover crypto news and analysis.

 •Join online communities, forums, and social media groups focused on cryptocurrencies. Engage in discussions and ask questions to learn from others in the space.

 •Attend conferences, webinars, and workshops to stay current with industry trends and network with experts and fellow investors.

By prioritising continuous learning and staying informed, you'll be well-equipped to adapt your strategy as the market evolves and make the most of your crypto investment journey.

Conclusion

Armed with a thorough understanding of the essentials of crypto investing, you're now prepared to embark on your journey in the digital asset world. In this guide, we have covered a wide range of topics, from the basics of cryptocurrency and blockchain technology to the key factors to consider when investing in cryptocurrencies. We hope that this guide has provided you with a solid foundation of knowledge and insights to help you make informed investment decisions in the dynamic world of cryptocurrencies.

As we have discussed throughout this guide, crypto investing can be a thrilling and potentially lucrative opportunity for investors willing to do their research, stay informed, and approach investing with patience and discipline. However, it's essential to recognise that cryptocurrency investing comes with risks and challenges, and there are no guarantees of returns.

To achieve success in cryptocurrency investing, it's crucial to have a solid investment strategy that aligns with your financial goals and risk tolerance. This means understanding the market trends, conducting thorough research on potential investments, and diversifying your portfolio to minimise your risk.

Moreover, it's important to take a responsible approach to cryptocurrency investing, which means taking the necessary precautions to secure your assets, adhering to sound investment principles, and being aware of the legal and regulatory landscape surrounding cryptocurrencies.

One of the most critical factors in successful cryptocurrency investing is staying informed and up-to-date with market trends, news, and developments. The cryptocurrency market is constantly evolving, and staying ahead of the curve can help you make better investment decisions and capitalise on emerging opportunities.

Additionally, it's crucial to have a solid understanding of the underlying technology behind cryptocurrencies, such as blockchain, to appreciate their potential and assess their viability as investments. As the technology and applications of cryptocurrencies continue to evolve, so too must your knowledge and understanding.

It's also important to recognise the potential for scams and fraudulent activity in the cryptocurrency space. While the blockchain technology that underpins cryptocurrencies is secure and transparent, there are still many bad actors in the space who may try to take advantage of investors. To protect yourself, it's essential to conduct thorough research on any potential investment opportunities, and to be wary of any promises of guaranteed returns or get-rich-quick schemes.

Despite these potential risks, the world of cryptocurrency investing is a vibrant and exciting one, with many opportunities for growth and innovation. Whether you're looking to invest in well-established cryptocurrencies like Bitcoin or exploring emerging altcoins, there is no shortage of investment opportunities in the space.

As you gain more experience and knowledge in the world of cryptocurrency investing, it's important to stay disciplined and focused on your long-term goals. This means avoiding the temptation to make impulsive investment decisions based on short-term market trends or emotions, and sticking to your investment plan even in the face of market volatility.

Crypto investing can be thrilling and rewarding, but it requires patience, caution, and a dedication to ongoing education. By following the guidance in this guide and staying informed, you'll be well on your way to a successful and responsible investment experience in the dynamic world of cryptocurrencies. Remember to approach investing with patience, caution, and a dedication to ongoing learning, and you'll be well-positioned to achieve your financial goals.

www.ingramcontent.com/pod-product-compliance
Lightning Source LLC
Chambersburg PA
CBHW040311220526
45473CB00002B/632